NATIONAL
GEOGRAPHIC

Better Off Wet

A Guide to Wetlands

Jeanne Weaver

Contents

Alligators and herons live ▶
together in this wetland.

Welcome to Wetlands

Can you guess what a **wetland** is? It is land that is soaked with water. Wetlands are like huge sponges. The ground and plants in a wetland soak up water. Many different kinds of plants and animals live in wetlands.

There are many types of wetlands. A wetland can be beside a river, lake, or ocean. A wetland can be a low spot in the woods or in a field. Some wetlands have trees. Others have grassy plants.

▼ Bog

n this book, you will visit a damp, spongy wetland called a **bog**. You will also see a **swamp**. A swamp s a wetland with trees. Finally, you will explore a grassy wetland called a **marsh**. Put on your ubber boots and let's go!

◀ Swamp

▼ Marsh

Bogs

When walking in a forest, you might find a wetland called a bog. Bogs are areas of wet ground that are covered with plants. The plants soak up the water and make the ground spongy.

A bog looks just like a small field in the forest. But watch out. Your shoes will get wet if you put your feet in this field.

▲ Cranberry bog

◄ Moss

Not many kinds of plants grow in bogs. The soil and water do not have the **nutrients** most plants need to grow. Cranberry plants can grow in a bog. The cranberry plant is a long tangle of green leaves and roots that spread over the water.

Tiny green plants called moss also grow in bogs. The moss grows thick like a carpet. When you stand on the thick moss, it jiggles and sways beneath your feet.

Bog Life

Lots of animals live in and around a bog. One animal that doesn't mind getting wet is the beaver. The beaver has an oily coating on its fur. When it crawls out of the bog, water drips off its fur. The beaver is dry right away.

▲ Beaver

▲ Spotted salamanders

The spotted salamander lives in a bog. It is safe from **predators** there. Fish eat salamander eggs, but very few fish live in bogs. A bog is the perfect place for the salamander to lay its eggs.

The snowshoe hare lives near bogs. It has big feet shaped like snowshoes. It can hop across the moss in a bog without sinking into the water.

▲ Snowshoe hare

9

Swamps

A swamp is a wetland that has woody plants like shrubs and trees. Cypress trees grow in swamps. They have special roots for swamp living. Cypress tree roots spread out far from the tree. This helps keep the tree stable in the muddy ground.

Some of the cypress trees' roots rise back up out of the water. Roots that do this are called "knees." Scientists think knees supply other tree roots with **oxygen** from the air.

Cypress tree roots ▶
that grow up out
of the water are
called "knees."

Swamp Life

A swamp is full of small animals like crayfish, frogs, and water beetles. A crayfish looks like a small lobster. Crayfish can survive when the swamp is dry because they can dig into the soil to find water.

▼ Crayfish

▲ Common frog

Many different kinds of frogs live in and around swamps. There is plenty of food in swamps for frogs. They eat insects, worms, and slugs.

Diving beetles also live in swamps. These beetles dive underwater for food. They eat snails and tiny fish. Diving beetles have a space under their wings to hold air while they are underwater.

▲ Diving beetle

Lots of big animals live in and around swamps. Alligators live in swamps. These animals may be large and dangerous, but they are a big help in a swamp.

◀ These alligators are resting in a gator hole.

As the swamp dries up, the alligator digs a deep hole in the mud. The "gator hole" holds water during dry weather. Turtles, shrimp, and fish live in the gator hole during the dry months. There would be very few fish in a swamp without gator holes.

▼Alligator

Marshes

A marsh is a wetland where grassy plants grow. Marshes can be found beside a river, lake, or ocean. Like a swamp, a marsh can be wet part of the time and dry part of the time.

The soil in a marsh has lots of nutrients. This means that many different kinds of plants can grow there. Cattails and reeds grow in marshes.

A cattail is a tall, narrow plant that can grow between four and nine feet high. Cattails can soak up lots of water and store it in their roots and stalks. Cattails are home to many types of birds and animals.

This bird has ▶ built its nest in the cattails.

Marsh Life

Lots of birds live in marshes. A marsh is a good home for the great blue heron. The heron wades in the shallow water on its long legs while it hunts for fish. Its long neck and beak allow it to snatch up a meal from the water.

▲ Great blue heron

▲ Great white egret

Snails ▶

The grassy plants in a marsh make a great resting place for birds. During fall, many birds **migrate**, or travel, south to warmer areas. In the spring, the birds migrate north again. Great white egrets stop to rest and feed in marshes when they migrate. They eat water plants and small animals such as snails and insects.

Better Off Wet

Wetlands provide homes and food for many different plants and animals. But they do more than that. Wetlands also help to prevent **floods**. The spongy ground and plants in a wetland soak up extra water when there are heavy rains. Areas with wetlands nearby have little flooding.

Wetlands also help keep our water clean. Sometimes waste from farms or factories **pollutes** the water in a river or stream. The polluted water is soaked up by the plants and thick soil in a wetland. When this happens, some of the pollution is taken out of the water.

It is important to protect wetlands. Many animals and plants rely on them for their home. People need wetlands because they help to prevent floods. They're also interesting places to visit. Wetlands are better off wet!

▼ You'll see things in a wetland you won't see anywhere else.

Glossary

bog   an area of wet, spongy ground

flood   water from a river or lake overflowing onto dry land

marsh   watery ground where grasses grow

migrate   to move from one place to another

nutrient   food that makes plants and animals grow

oxygen   a gas in the air that plants and animals need to live

pollute   to make dirty

predator   an animal that eats other animals

swamp   watery land where woody plants like trees and shrubs grow

wetland   an area of land that is soaked with water

Index